Living in Ancient Egypt

On the banks of the Nile,
in the days of the pharaohs . . .

Over three thousand years ago, there lived in Egypt a peaceful, learned people. They loved building beautiful houses, and magnificent temples and palaces. Over the centuries, desert sand has blown over and into their buildings, burying them and hiding them from sight.

For Alice

Written by Corinne Courtalon
Illustrated by Christian Broutin

Specialist adviser: George Hart,
The British Museum

ISBN 1 85103 038 7
First published 1988 in the United Kingdom by
Moonlight Publishing Ltd,
131 Kensington Church Street, London W8

© *1986 by Editions Gallimard*
Translated by Sarah Matthews
English text © *1988 by Moonlight Publishing Ltd*
Printed in Italy by La Editoriale Libraria

How can we find out how the Ancient Egyptians lived? By patiently clearing away the sand. This is what archaeologists do to find statues, furniture, pottery, paintings, and even golden treasure, all left behind by the Ancient Egyptians. This study is called Egyptology.

If you go to museums like the British Museum in London, or the Metropolitan in New York, you will see some of the Ancient Egyptian objects which have been rescued from the sand.

It is very hot in Egypt. Most of the country is covered in desert, where rain hardly ever falls, nothing can grow, and no one can live.

There are gazelle and lion in the desert. Other strange creatures lurk there too: scarab beetles, scorpions, vultures, vipers. A scorpion sting may kill a small child.

Egypt is in
North-east
Africa.

The Nile valley is
shown in green.

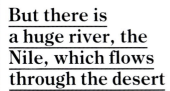

**But there is
a huge river, the
Nile, which flows
through the desert**
for 6700 kilometres. The Ancient
Egyptians live along the riverbank.
The river gives them water, and
makes the ground damp for crops. In
the summer, the sun becomes so hot it
seems everything will burn up. But
then the Nile swells with water
and overflows its banks into the valley.
Three months later, it goes down.

**In summer the valley is flooded. The river brings thick, fertile
mud which it leaves along the banks as it goes down.**

**In winter, the river stays in its bed. In the rich, water-soaked
soil of the valley, plants can grow.**

Boats travel up and down the Nile: boats with sails, boats with oars carrying goods, and little ferry-boats flitting from one side of the river to the other. Fishermen make themselves very light small boats from the papyrus reeds which grow along the riverbank. The pharaoh and his court travel in beautiful painted boats with rows and rows of oars.

Hunters kill duck and geese with throwing-sticks a little like boomerangs.

The river is teeming with fish:
eels, carp, catfish, tench. The Egyptians
make a sort of caviare from
mullet-eggs. But there are crocodiles
in the river too, and hippopotami. They
can sometimes tip over a boat and
sink it. Noblemen enjoy going out on
hippopotamus hunts with ropes and
harpoons. And on the riverbank there are
cobras - their bite can kill!

The crown of the
Southern Kingdom

The crown of the
Northern Kingdom

The crown of Egypt

The pharaoh is a very powerful king.

The Egyptians believe that he is
the son of the sun, and that he has
supernatural powers. They call him
God-King. What does he look like?
Around the temples are huge statues
of the pharaohs, like the one in the
picture on the left. Often he wears a
headcloth over his wig: the nemes. On
his chin he has a false beard, and on
his forehead the uraeus.
This is a little model
cobra which protects
the king.

The pharaoh wears a kepresh
on his head.

The queen

The prince is
holding a
lotus-flower.

There are crowds of servants to wait on the pharaoh.

Friendly nations bring expensive presents for him.

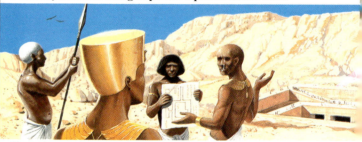

He orders palaces, tombs and temples to be built.

The pharaoh likes to go lion-hunting in his chariot.

Egypt is a rich and
fertile land, and for
a while the Egyptians
were content to stay within
its boundaries. Gradually,
though, they moved further
and further afield, earning
a reputation as **famous warriors**.

Prisoners

Under the pharaohs they have conquered a
great empire stretching from Syria to the
Sudan. The army is huge and well-
organised. The prisoners-of-war are taken
to work as servants, or in gold-mines or
quarries in the desert. One day, though, the
Egyptians themselves will be beaten.
Powerful peoples from across the desert,
like the Nubians and the Persians, or from
the shores of the Mediterranean Sea, like
the Greeks and Romans, will in turn
overrun the Egyptian empire.

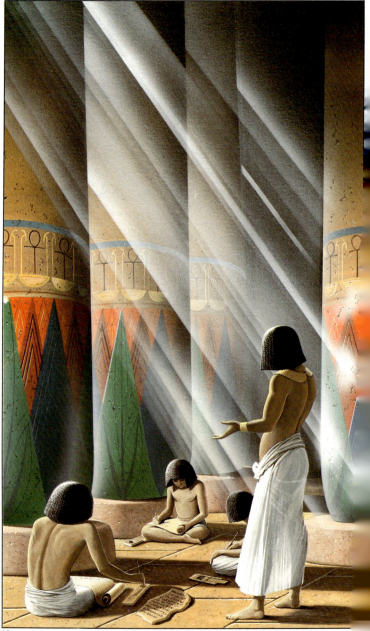

This is some Egyptian writing.

Scribes help the pharaoh.

They are very important, because they can read and write. They are sent all over Egypt to keep watch over the harvests and the building of the temples. Occasionally they make expeditions into the desert to bring back precious metals and jewels.

How can you become a scribe?

By learning to read, write and count. You start on clay tablets, then, when you are good enough, you can write with pen and ink on a fine roll of **papyrus**, or paper. Because it rolls up it is easy to carry around and store.

Papyrus is a plant which grows near the Nile. The stalk is trimmed, then stripped and flattened to make paper.

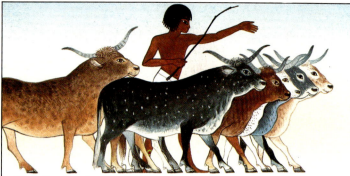

After the floods, the fields are sown. Cattle are led over the fields to tread the seeds deep into the mud.

Water from the Nile must be taken to the fields, to help the crops grow.

The peasants use a shadoof. A sort of bucket on one end of a pole is balanced by a weight on the other. The pole swings round from the river to tip water into the irrigation canals. The harvests are rich in Ancient Egypt. You can see on the page on the right a scribe watching the harvest.

Hoe

Carpenter's tool

Knife   Awl

The Egyptians wear a lot of make-up. They put black kohl all round their eyes to protect them from the glare of the sun.

They love going up on to the flat roofs of their houses to chat in the cool of the evening.

What do the Egyptians wear?

The men wear a linen kilt, the women a long linen dress, while the children often don't wear anything at all. Rich Egyptians wear heavy wigs to show how important they are. The women's wigs are longer than the men's and have turquoise or gold beads braided in the ends.

Mirror

What are their houses like?

They are built of mud bricks, then painted in bright colours. They have flat roofs, often with silos on them to store the grain. In the gardens, papyrus and sycamores grow around a pool.

The Egyptians love cats. They train them to go hunting. A lot of cats are even mummified after they die.

Make-up spoon

Bracelet

Sandals

Look at these household objects.
They're not very different from ours...

Egyptians eat their meals sitting round a low table. They sit on the ground or on low stools. They drink beer out of cups, and don't use plates. Everyone just picks what they want out of the dish with their fingers. What do they eat? Above all, fish, onions and bread, but also birds, beef, lettuce, lentils, cucumbers, dates. . .

The Egyptians make things out of wood: chairs, tables, and wooden head-rests which they use as pillows. The rich have ornamented beds with carved legs. They have beautiful jewellery made from gold and precious stones.

Skimmers

Sieve

Broom

Chair

Head-rest

Bed

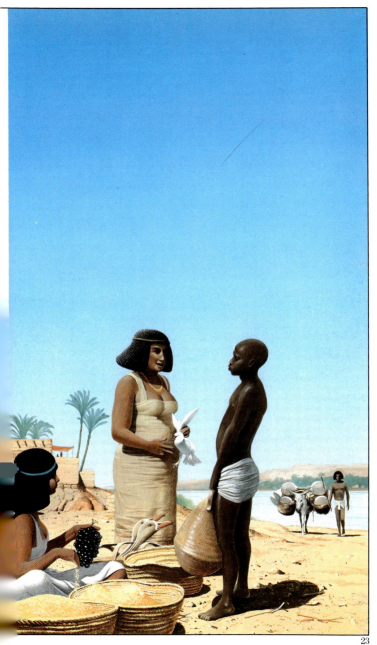

The Egyptians love family life.
They particularly like playing games
together: dice, knuckle-bones,
checkers, and a game like
snakes-and-ladders called senet.
**The very rich organise splendid
feasts for their friends.** On their
heads they wear cones of scented
grease which melt and drip down
their faces, cooling them pleasantly
as the party wears on! There is an
orchestra, and dancers to amuse the
guests. The musicians play the harp,
the lute, and the flute. The dancers
beat time with small rattles called
sistra.

Children's toys: a leopard with a mouth that opens, a pull-along horse on wheels, a doll

Boys and girls prefer more active games: shooting arrows at targets, wrestling, or a game rather like our piggy-back. Little children have lovely toys made out of wood and fabric: spinning tops, balls, dolls, and animals on wheels to pull along.

A ball game

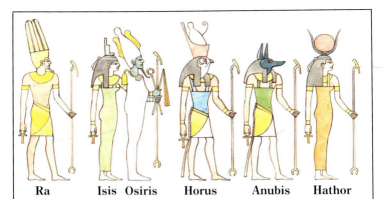

Ra   Isis Osiris   Horus   Anubis   Hathor

Who are all these people with animal heads or strange crowns?

They are the gods who watch over the Egyptians. They each have their own great temples. Nobody is allowed in except the priests. Each god has his own statue deep in the most secret room of his temple. Sometimes, on feast days, the statues of the gods are carried out and the priests and people walk with them in long processions.

The two enormous stone needles standing at the front of the temple are called obelisks.

Have you heard of the Pyramids of Egypt? They stand in the desert, safely away from the Nile floods. They are gigantic tombs. Inside each pyramid is a maze of secret galleries leading to the room where the pharaoh's mummy in its coffin lies hidden.

Pyramid of Cheops:
1 - Chamber of the king
2 - Store-room
3 - Unfinished chamber
4 - Great gallery

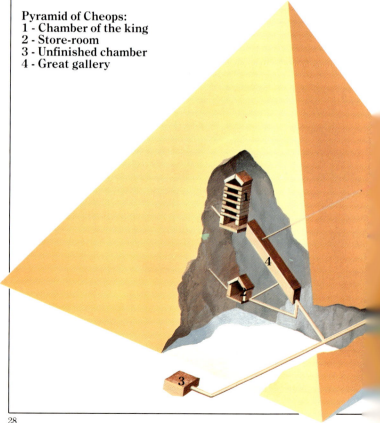

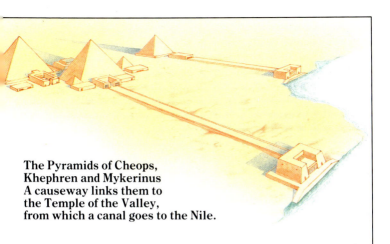

The Pyramids of Cheops,
Khephren and Mykerinus
A causeway links them to
the Temple of the Valley,
from which a canal goes to the Nile.

Next to the burial chamber are rooms filled with furniture, vases and precious things: **the pharaoh's treasures.** The pyramid has been designed so that it's almost impossible to get inside once the pharaoh has been buried.
The entrance is hidden and the galleries leading to the king's burial chamber are blocked off to stop grave-robbers. The highest Egyptian pyramid of all is the tomb of Cheops: it is a hundred and forty-six metres high.

It can take over thirty years to build a pyramid. First the stone has to be fetched. Some stones are close by in the desert, but others, like granite, have to come from quarries far away. It must be loaded on to boats and floated down the Nile. Then it is dragged on rollers to the place where the pyramid is to be built.

Some of the blocks of stone weigh over twenty tons, and without any cranes it seems impossible to lift them up to build the pyramid walls. So the Egyptians make huge ramps of brick all around the pyramid. Then the stone can be hauled right up to the top. The pharaoh makes the peasants do this sort of work. The pyramids rise up into the sky, showing the greatness of the dead pharaohs—
and of the living Egypt.

When somebody dies, the body is embalmed to preserve it and stop it rotting away. A body preserved like this is called a mummy.

The body is perfumed and wrapped in bandages.

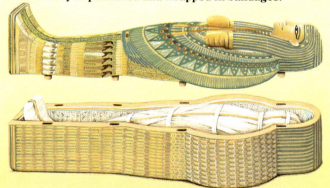

The mummy is put inside a beautiful wooden coffin.

In the desert, there are tombs dug out of the mountainsides.
They are like real houses, with lots of rooms. The Ancient Egyptians believe there is a life after death. So that the dead person will be happy in the land of the dead, the walls are painted with pictures of the Nile, of the animals and people living along its banks, and of happy moments in the dead person's life. The rooms are filled with beautiful furniture and shabtis are put all around the mummy. What are shabtis? They are little statues of servants for the dead person. The most thoughtful provide three hundred and sixty-five shabtis – one for each day of the year!

◄ The dead live in another world, protected by the god Anubis and ruled over by Osiris.

To get to the desert, where the dead are buried, the bodies have to be carried across the Nile.

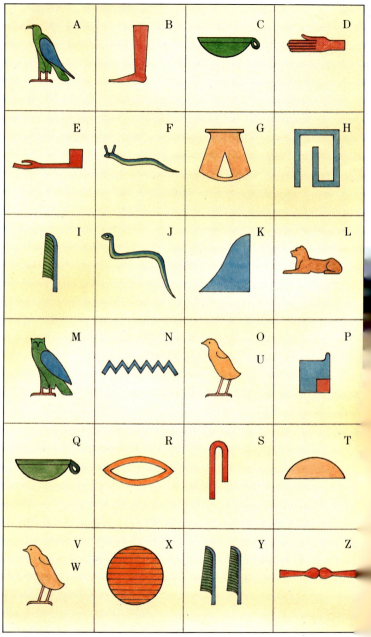

Writing with pictures

Egyptian writing was done in a series of little drawings of things, plants and animals. These are **hieroglyphs.** Archaeologists have found some of them carved on the walls of temples or at the base of statues; others were written on papyrus or painted on walls.

What do they mean? The meaning of hieroglyphs took a long time to rediscover. In the end, in 1822, a Frenchman called Champollion studied a stone with the same thing written in Egyptian hieroglyphs and in two languages which he already knew – modern Egyptian and Ancient Greek. He used the familiar languages to work out the meaning of the hieroglyphs. At last people had the key to the lost civilisation of Ancient Egypt.

If you were a girl, your name would be followed by the picture of a woman; a boy's name was followed by the picture of a man.

Index